Gustave Courbet: Exposed

Edited By Lacey Belinda Smith

Gustave Courbet (1819-77) was a French painting and sculpture. He started and dominated the French movement toward realism. Best known as an innovator in Realism (and credited with coining the term). He bridged the gap between Romanticism and the Impressionist school of painters.

Torso of a Woman

The painter's atelier, Detail

Femme Nue

Gypsy in Reflection

La Sieste 2

Portrait of Laure Borreau

Lot and His Daughters—1844

Bather Sleeping by a Brook
Romanticism

Female Nude with a Dog (Portrait of Leotine Renaude)
Realism

La Bacchante

Nude Reclining by the Sea
Romanticism

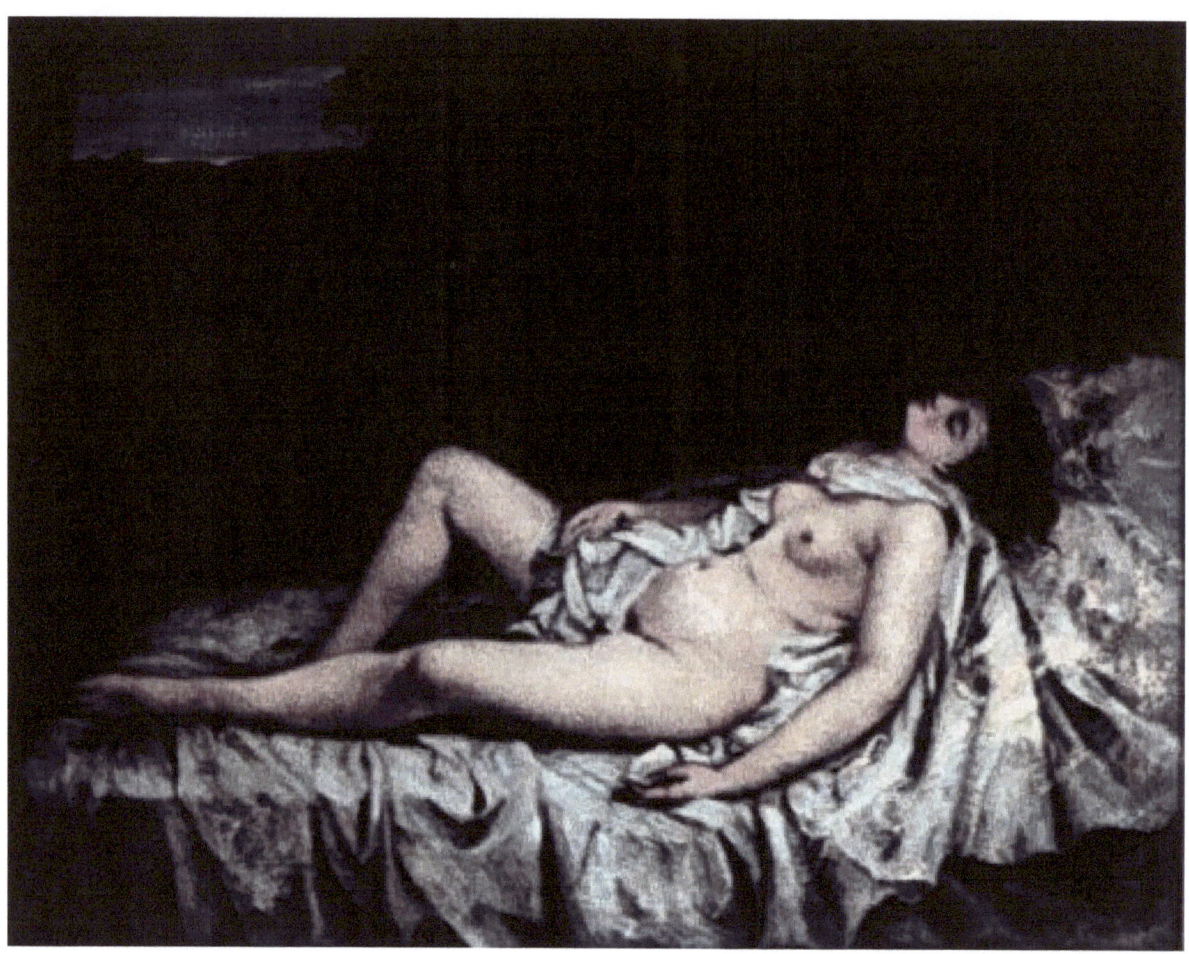

Reclining nude

Sleeping Nude

The Source

The Young Bather

The Bathers--1858

Woman with white stockings

Sleeping Nude Woman

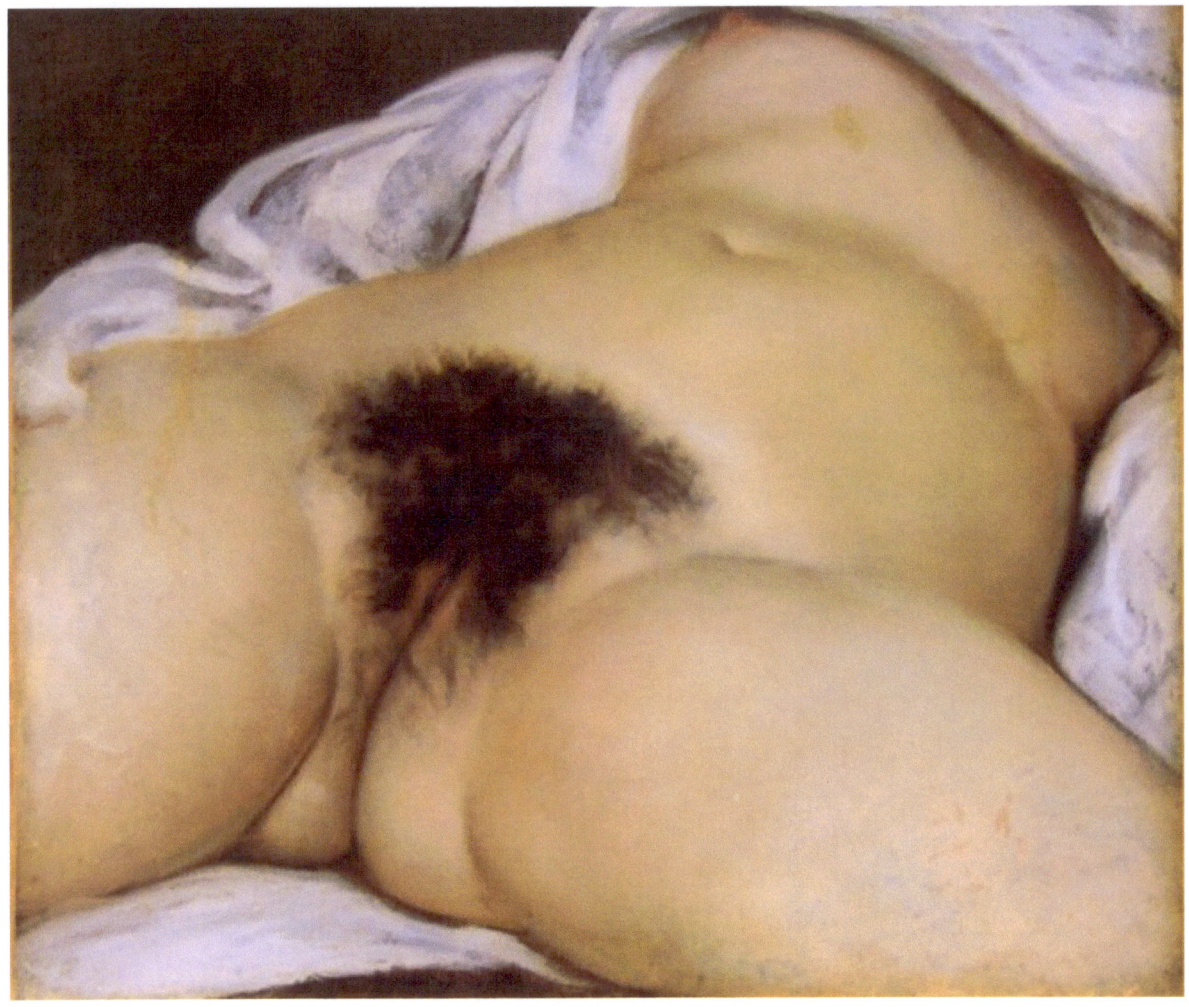

The Origin of the World --1866
Realism

The Sleepers -- 1866
Realism

Woman with a Parrot

The Source (Bather at the Source) --1868

The Woman in the Waves (The Bather) --1868

L'atelier du peintre—1855